The
GOLFER'S
GUIDE *to the*
MEANING *of* LIFE

Titles in the
GUIDES *to the* MEANING *of* LIFE
series

The Runner's Guide to the Meaning of Life

The GOLFER'S GUIDE *to the* MEANING *of* LIFE

LESSONS I'VE LEARNED
FROM MY LIFE ON THE LINKS

BY GARY PLAYER

WINNER OF MORE THAN 160 PROFESSIONAL TOURNAMENTS,
INCLUDING THE GRAND SLAM OF GOLF

Skyhorse Publishing

www.skyhorsepublishing.com

Library of Congress Cataloging-in-Publication Data is available on file.

ISBN-10: 1-60239-255-2
ISBN-13: 978-1-60239-255-7

10 9 8 7 6 5 4 3 2 1

Printed in China.

To my wife Vivienne and children
Jennifer, Marc, Wayne, Michele, Theresa,
and Amanda

Contents

Why Play Golf?

When I was a boy in South Africa, I attended King Edward VII School in Johannesburg. My mother died when I was just eight years old. At the time, my father was busy working in the gold mines; my brother was off fighting in World War II alongside the British, Americans, and Canadians; and my sister was off at boarding school. I was alone a lot of the time, and my extracurricular activities at King Edward VII were often my only source of entertainment and amusement. I played *everything*—soccer, rugby, cricket. I ran sprints and jumped hurdles. I was a springboard diver, and I participated in gymnastics. Sports and competition were my passion.

Eventually, my father took me out for my first round of golf on a course owned by one of the gold mining companies. I made pars on the first three holes I ever played. They were very easy holes, of course, but it didn't matter: I was hooked. The golf swing came very naturally to me, similar as it is to the one used in cricket.

As soon as I began playing golf on a regular basis, I came to a realization that I have been thankful for ever since. When I played golf, I realized, I was not subjecting my body to absurd amounts of abuse and punishment. Yes, I liked to push my body to keep fit, but only in a healthy way and on my terms. The fact that a person could be maimed and crocked (as we say in South Africa) for the rest of his life by playing rugby or football or by boxing was not lost on me. High-speed collisions of human bodies and constant thumping on my brain,

I knew, would eventually affect the quality of my life and probably shorten it as well.

It was this realization that led me to pursue golf, instead of the other sports of my youth, full time. Today, I am still going to the gym, pumping iron, watching my diet, working on my mental toughness, and trying to win golf championships. In fact, as these words are written, I am on a quest to win a professional golf tournament in a sixth consecutive decade. I have won major championships in the 1950s, '60s, '70s, '80s, and '90s, yet, at the age of 65, I play on. This longevity reflects who I am, but more so, it reflects the graciousness of the game of golf. Golf truly opens its arms to all and gives you a lifelong opportunity to rise up, excel, and enjoy.

My years in golf have taught me another fundamental truth. Any person's life is enriched by the passionate pursuit of something. And in my mind, the best passions are those that last for a whole lifetime.

That makes most sports challenging passions to embrace. I'm sure you'll agree that there is

nothing sadder than to come in contact with people
who feel that their glory days are behind them, left
on the high school football field 30 years ago or on
the university baseball diamond. Even at the highest
levels of most sports—the place where people such
as Michael Jordan, Willie Mays, and Joe Montana
performed—the game leaves them in the lurch by
their mid-30s. Joe Montana cannot get the same
thrill out of playing catch that he did out of winning
the Super Bowl. Michael Jordan cannot get the
same spark from a pickup game that he did from
winning the NBA Championship. And they are
both still young men. People don't realize what a
person goes through mentally once he realizes his
body will no longer allow him to do the thing he
loves most. It certainly must cause various forms of
depression.

The passion we call our own takes on sundry
versions for every person. It need not be athletic, although that is what I understand best. The important thing is to *have* that passion and to make sure it's
one without time limitations attached to it. The

possibilities for such a passion are plentiful. You can learn to play the piano no matter how old you are. You can develop an appreciation for gardening at any time and pursue it until you draw your final breath. You can even make a passion out of learning to cook gourmet (and healthy!) meals for you and your family, or of collecting and reading all of the classic writings known to man. All of these things are passions you cannot exhaust.

If your interests lie in the areas of sport and competition, however, golf can provide you with passion and longevity that know no peer in the world of sport. In other sports, athletes are over the hill by the time they reach their mid-30s. In golf, a fellow is just reaching his prime by this age, and that prime can continue for many more years. That includes you too, my friend. Even if you could hit the golf ball farther when you were 18 or 25, you weren't nearly as smart a player as you are now. You didn't have the acquired knowledge of successes and failures that you now have. Whatever age you are, you have the potential to be playing golf better than you ever have! Despite my years, I feel as if I just started playing the game. And I plan to keep on going for at least another 20 years. The challenge is still there and *I can still respond to it.*

Golf rewards you with the healthful side effects of long walks (and you should walk when you play) without the high-impact, downside risks you take with your physical well-being in other sports. The game of golf challenges your mind anew every single day and presents you with the ultimate opponent: yourself. I've always been amazed that people can derive so much satisfaction out of beating others when they have never taken the ultimate test of battling themselves.

It doesn't make sense to pursue any game other than golf when you consider that it will present you with the greatest mental and physical challenge of your life as far as difficulty is concerned, and that it will keep you entertained as long as you can get out of bed in the morning.

One of my heroes in life is Mother Teresa, the sainted nun of Calcutta. I remember reading about someone years ago asking her the question: Why do you live your life as you do? Her answer: "Why would I do otherwise?"

As to the question of "Why play golf?" I would suggest a similar answer. Why *not* play golf? Anyone can do it, and, as you will find out in the following pages, the rewards to the mind and the soul are endless.

Success

I was just 17 years old when I decided to become a professional golfer. Two things motivated me at the time: competition and money. I yearned for the former—I still do to this day—and one must have money to survive. Even though the prize money available to a professional golfer in the mid-1950s was paltry, it seemed like a lot to a 17-year-old boy. Armed mostly with an excess of determination, I set off down an unknown path.

Determination is a curious emotion. It can be cultivated to some degree, but largely, it is something you possess when you are born. Determination has always come naturally to me, but I think my difficult childhood enhanced it.

As a young professional, I had a slightly unorthodox swing. Specifically, the position of my left wrist at the top of my backswing was what is known as flat or laid off. In English, that means it bent away from the back of my head rather than cupping toward my head. This was a fairly minor thing in the grand scheme of the golf swing, but it was the focal point whenever I was singled out for criticism or my swing was analyzed by an "expert." Such criticism simply made me more determined.

And what, pray tell, was I determined to do? The great Ben Hogan had always said that the secret to golf was in the dirt. I thought that he was probably correct, so I initially used my determination to fuel a practice regimen that was as grueling as one could undertake in golf. I lived and practiced at a golf course in the South African countryside called Virginia Park. Like any golf course, it was filled with people on weekends but nearly deserted during the week. I used those weekdays to full advantage. I arose at 6:00 A.M. and hit piles and piles of practice balls until breakfast time. After breakfast, I returned to my practice until lunchtime. After lunch, I took a lie-down for 30 minutes or so, and when I woke up, I went back to the golf course until it was dark. When I went home, I continued working on my game by swinging a club on a rubber mat inside the house.

Month in and month out, I practiced and hit as many balls as is humanly possible. I had lifted weights from my early boyhood years, and I continued to do so even though conventional wisdom in golf stated that bulky muscles were bad for a golfer's swing. That wisdom may have been correct to some degree, but I knew that the correct muscles tuned in the proper way would give me an advantage over players who ignored their bodies. So I continued to move the iron.

Looking back, there have been other golfers who practiced and worked as hard as I did—I can remember, for example, my fascination with how hard Arnold Palmer practiced when I saw him on my first trip to America—but never one who worked harder.

I mention this because in today's world, both golf and otherwise, it has become the norm for people to look for easy answers. People want success without effort, reward without work. There are a lot of people who feel as if something is owed to them, whether that something is monetary wealth, peace of mind, or respect. I don't mind telling you that people with that attitude make me sick.

In my days as a professional golfer, I've seen a lot of hotshot young players come along with more God-given talent than any man has a right to possess. On almost every count, I've seen them come well short of fulfilling their potential because they mistakenly believed that talent alone would make them a champion. Today, young Tiger Woods is trampling the competition in professional golf. Tiger has loads of talent, but the thing that makes him a champion is that he *outworks* every other player in the game. He practices harder and smarter and longer than all the rest. If ever there was a golfer entitled to feel as if he could "get by" on talent alone, it is Tiger Woods. He eschews this notion, however, because he realizes that no one is born with an entitlement to being the best.

Those who believe that talent is enough to guarantee their best possible performance are destined to fail. An attorney with a facile mind is no match for an opponent who is thoroughly prepared. A salesman who thinks that his product alone is good enough to make every sale is certain to lose sales because he has not familiarized himself with the needs of his potential customers. They have not practiced. They have not prepared to succeed.

There is an interesting corollary to the idea that winning can only come through determination and hard work. There are some who would suggest that to win at anything—to make the big sale, win the big case, make the big putt—one must be blessed with a little bit of luck at precisely the right moment in time. I know for a fact that in my own career, the harder I worked, the "luckier" I got. There is no such thing as dumb luck. There are dumb people who presume at some point that something lucky will happen, and there are determined people who presume nothing will happen unless they *make it happen*. The dumb ones call these people lucky.

A friend of mine who is a writer once told me that he has met hundreds of people who, upon hearing his occupation, respond, "I've always wanted to be a writer." He didn't have to tell me the rest of the story. The reason he is a successful writer and those other people aren't is due only in small part to talent. He did, however, put a thought into words that I'd never really heard before: *Simply by making the effort to start something, you will be miles ahead of almost everyone else.* After that, the key to success lies in your determination to see it through and your willingness to outwork the few who have chosen the same path.

If you devote just 1 hour a week to practicing your golf game, you will see some improvement, and you will make more progress than people who don't practice. If you can spare several hours to practice, the improvement will be exponential. In that microcosm, golf tells the story of life: We all seek the keys to success, but success does not look for us. We must pursue it. When the pursuit is fueled by determination and hard work, things fall into place with remarkable ease.

THE ESSENTIAL TRAITS
OF A GOLFER

I speak often about how determination and hard work are the keys to success. However, there are other traits that are fundamental to golf mastery. And as usual, they apply well to all aspects of living. Here are five important ones.

PATIENCE

There is not a single passionate pursuit that does not require patience, and yet it seems such a difficult thing for most people to exercise. When the topic is patience, I always think of Jack Nicklaus, the man who has won more major championships than any golfer in history. He realized that it is the deadly sin of golf to try to force the issue with overly aggressive play. He also recognized that under pressure, most people cannot resist the temptation to make something happen. Jack's tactic when he was near the lead was to simply wait things out—let the others make the mistakes, and let the titles come to him. His trophy case tells a book's worth of tales about patience.

RESILIENCY

Most of the people who play golf do not play it very well. If I had to pick a single reason why, I would say it is the inability of their spirit to bounce back from adverse occurrences. That is a sorry state of mind to take onto the golf course because golf is nothing if not a journey of adversity. Even the best player seldom executes a shot precisely the way he hopes he will. This means that with nearly every shot we play, we are challenged to find the positive side of it and continue the fight toward our end goal. Life is not lived by going into seclusion when fate goes against us. It is lived by meeting failure head on, learning from it, and using it to prepare for future success.

CLARITY

There is an old saying in golf regarding the inability to perform when we overanalyze a situation: "Paralysis by analysis." This condition occurs when we lose sight of the simple goal of golf—to hole the ball in as few strokes as possible—and instead become wrapped up in the idea of "how" we do each aspect of the game. The vast majority of people would have you believe that we live in a world of ever-increasing complexity and that demands on time make it nearly impossible to focus on doing any one thing well. The truth is that we foist this idea of complex lives upon ourselves. Life— and golf as a reflection of it—remains simple if you can only manage to keep an unclouded view of where it is you're going. We fail to arrive at our goals when we allow ourselves to be distracted from looking at them from an unobstructed point of view. We humans are remarkable in our ability to invent distractions. If a player like Lee Trevino or myself had worried about how we looked swinging the club, or how making a par from a bunker wasn't as good as a par when we hit the green and two-putted, we would never have made it in professional golf. The purpose in striving is to get the thing done, not to worry about *how* you get the thing done.

CURIOSITY

The key to learning about anything in life is to be curious about everything. Golf offers us the chance to satisfy our curiosity in a variety of ways. The most obvious is by traveling to play courses we haven't seen before. Any golfer can eventually play well if he plays the same golf course over and over. We can only prove to ourselves that we have truly improved our game, however, by taking our game on the road, so to speak. Are we capable of playing a course with narrow fairways and tall rough? Or lightning fast greens? Or the windy, bouncy game of the links? This notion of curiosity is taken a step further by entering competitions. No matter what level of golf you play, there is always a competition available to you at the club, local, and state levels. To avoid playing in them is to push curiosity into the corner and to never learn the things about yourself that competition reveals to us. Embracing the revelations that are brought to us by curiosity serves to enrich our lives.

TALENT

It might strike you as a bit unfair that I list talent as an essential trait for a golfer, but the truth is we all have it. Some have varying degrees of physical talent; some have varying degrees of mental talent. The point is that you definitely have some talent. The objective in golf is to know your talents and to determine how you can use them to improve your game. By knowing where your talents lie, you can always play to your strengths. This makes any pursuit easier and more fun because our strengths tend to correlate with our interests—our head, therefore, stays in the game. If your talents are mental, you are not at a disadvantage against the physically talented person. You can plan and prepare better than he can, you can outthink him during the contest, and you can manage your game better. The idea here is to know what you're good at and to focus on getting as much out of those assets as you possibly can.

Learning

**WHY SELF-EDUCATION
IS THE BEST EDUCATION**

I can still visualize it as if it had happened last week. It was 1957, and I was on my first trip to America. I can remember the excitement at coming to a country that I admired so much, a country for which I knew that all others turned to in times of trouble. I knew from reading the speeches of Sir Winston Churchill that during the darkest hours of the early years of World War II—the 2 years before America entered the war—he had beseeched free men to have faith in America. In one of his finest moments of oration, just after the United States passed the Lend-Lease Act, Churchill had ended one of his speeches with these words from a rather obscure poem by Arthur Hugh Clough:

> And not by eastern windows only,
> When daylight comes, comes in the light;
> In front the sun climbs slow, how slowly,
> But westward, look, the land is bright.

For me and millions of others like me, America was a symbol of opportunity, the place where I could make my mark on the world.

The professional golf tour in America at the time was home to the world's best players. In my very first tournament at the Seminole Golf Club in Florida, I was paired with the man who already had influenced the way I practiced and played: the legendary Ben Hogan. Now, Hogan was feared by most other players because they misunderstood his intensity to be a sign that he didn't like them. The truth was he didn't notice them—or anyone else! He was completely absorbed in his own game. Before we started the round, I mentioned to him that I'd just come from England where I'd won a tournament, but that already I had critics who said I would never last as a professional golfer because my swing was too flat. He looked directly at me and said, "Your swing can never be too flat."

That was about the extent of our conversation, but right there I had learned something. Here was the greatest ball striker in the world telling me not to worry about what people said. Many of the alleged experts thought that the only way to win golf tournaments was with a great golf swing. At a time in life when I was still not fully mature in terms of self-confidence, there was a danger I would believe that sort of stuff. With those simple words from Hogan, I learned something: The swing is not the thing. The professional tours were and still are loaded with people who can swing the golf club as gracefully as you please. That does not make them great players. The difference between being a good swinger of the club and a great player lies between the ears, in the mind. To keep your mind open to learning new things is to keep progressing forward in life.

After that round of golf with Ben Hogan, I watched him hit balls for 3 solid hours. He never took a break, and I never took my eyes off him. I knew he wasn't much for conversation, so I decided I would take the opportunity to learn from him simply by watching. I remember being amazed at how low he hit the ball—his ballflight was that of a low, boring missile. The ball crackled off the clubface.

A few years later, I saw Jack Nicklaus play for the first time and was amazed at how astonishingly high he hit the ball. That confirmed it for me: Golf was a game of wild contradictions. It was the mind and heart that got things done.

Those early years in America taught me that if I was going to learn things, I couldn't depend on others to learn them for me (the critics) or to teach me (my fellow players, although they were always gracious). I realized that my education would come from observing and soaking in new experiences and the varying individual approaches to getting things done. I found that the trick to learning was to keep my eyes open as much as my ears, perhaps even more so.

Soon, my travels extended to the entire world. Whether in India or parts of Africa where I had not been before, I always noticed the foods people ate. In general, they didn't eat a lot of butter, meat, cream, bacon, or white bread. There was almost a complete absence of the refined foods that I saw in Western places. Yet these people were fit and strong as oxen, able to work all day long. There was something to be learned from that, and I didn't have to ask anyone what it was. As a result, I made adjustments to my own diet, which I follow to this day.

In retrospect, I realize it would have been easy for me to assume that as a young professional golfer on the rise, I knew most of what I needed to know about the game and about life. I'm sure I had moments when I thought that very thing. And if I had kept thinking that way, it would have been a horrific mistake for me. Luckily, I saw so much that it was impossible for me to ignore. I was open-minded enough to realize that these other fellows were pretty good at what they did, and that they might know a thing or two that never occurred to me no matter how much I thought I knew about becoming a better player.

Once I opened my mind to new things, I realized that I must keep it open, that I must look upon life as a continual learning process. Those who fail to realize this remain stuck in the same place their entire lives.

Your mind is just like your body. The more you exercise it, the better it works. There is only one way to exercise your mind: Use it. The only way to use it is to constantly feed it with new information, things it has not been fed before. If you open your eyes, they will open your mind to new things. Once you start, it will be just like physical exercise: The more dedicated you are to learning, the more you will learn.

Gratitude

THE FULFILLMENT

GAINED BY GIVING BACK

The 1962 U.S. Open Championship is re-membered by golf fans for the famous duel it pro-duced between Arnold Palmer and the young Jack Nicklaus. Jack ultimately won the tournament—his first victory as a professional golfer—at the expense of Arnold, who was by then the most popular and dominant golfer in America.

I remember that championship clearly, as well, but for different reasons than most. I felt I had a chance to win and was so disappointed not to. While walking up to the final hole, I turned to Joe Dey, then director of the United States Golf Association (USGA). I conveyed my disappointment and said, "Had I won, Joe, I planned on giving the prize money to charity, especially to cancer research. But let's keep that a secret. One day I shall win, and I'll turn back the money to a good cause. That is a promise."

That day came 3 years later at Bellerive Country Club in St. Louis, when I won the U.S. Open in an 18-hole playoff with the Australian Kel Nagle. Upon being presented the winner's check, I handed it back to Joe Dey and told him that a portion of it should go to cancer research and that the rest should go to the development of junior golf programs by the USGA.

In 1965, $25,000 was a very considerable sum of money, and it was certainly one of the biggest prizes I had won up to that point. Giving it away, I must say, felt wonderful beyond words. And that's my point here. I tell this story not to paint myself as a generous man, but rather to stress the enormous satisfaction that can be derived from giving something back to the world in moments of success.

My mother died from cancer, and I always had it in my mind that I would one day honor her in such a fashion. As for the junior golf part of the donation, I long remembered the words of my biggest hero, Sir Winston Churchill, who said, "The youth of a nation are the trustees of posterity." In my mind, that donation to junior golf was a small way of paying a debt that all free men owe to that great man.

Playing the game of golf from the time I was a young man provided me with continual lessons in gratitude and the notion that we must constantly be aware of our responsibility to give of ourselves. The integrity of the game of golf has survived untainted for something like 600 years because the idea of guardianship of the game's spirit is so imbedded in the simple playing of the game. When we rip a chunk of sod out of the ground with an iron shot, we are careful to find the bit of earth and replace it. We do this as a courtesy to those who will come along after us on the golf course. If those playing ahead of us do not afford us the same courtesy, our enjoyment of the game is lessened. But they *do* afford us that same courtesy.

The same idea is apparent when a player's ball is in a sand bunker and he goes in to play it. He makes a real mess of things, leaving footprints all over the place and a small pit at the point where his club entered the sand behind the ball. Before moving on, the player carefully smoothes over the sand with a rake. It would be easier not to, but he has a responsibility to the people who will come after him to do so.

This idea that we, as golfers, each look after the ones who come behind us extends obviously to other areas of our lives. The act of replacing a divot or smoothing over a bunker is a simple thing, but it serves to remind us that no matter what we do in life and no matter at what stage of life we are, we owe a debt to those who came before us and to those who come after us. We have all benefited from those who came before us—our parents, our teachers, and those who long before us took the same path we aspire to. To acknowledge them in your mind is to understand that no man gets where he's going without the help of others.

Your instincts should tell you that just as they helped you, you must help others. The opportunities to do so are endless. In the business world, the opportunity to mentor a young person just out of college is a way to change that young person's life—and your own. The pride that can be derived from knowing someone considers you a mentor is beyond quantifying. And the impact your efforts make can be the beginning of a string of events in that person's life that otherwise might never have occurred. The realization of their dreams can act as a completion of the circle of life's responsibilities for you.

I have never stopped being grateful for the influence my schooling had on me in the early years of my life. When I purchased my ranch, Blair Atholl, in South Africa, it came with the responsibility of keeping up a school for the local black children. Many of them were deprived of a good education during the apartheid era, and I wanted to make a difference in their lives. Today, two schools stand just a few hundred yards from my home. There is a nursery school for more than 100 children and a primary school for more than 300 students. The school provides these kids with the highest possible standard of education, gives them a sense of dress code, and allows them to say a prayer of their own faith, no matter their religion (or lack thereof). We feed the children every day, the teachers and their families live on the property, and we've even built a soccer stadium and a computer resource center for the kids. In my travels around the world, I continually raise money for The Player Foundation, which supports the schools. Sometimes I drop by the schools and sing with the children. Other times, I go to watch their soccer games against other schools.

Occasionally, when I'm hitting practice balls on the ranch, a few of the students will wander up and sit and watch a spell. Mind you, I'm only practicing, and I'm just hitting golf balls like I have for thousands of days in my life. When those kids watch, they clap for me each time I hit the ball. Such moments never fail to bring a tear to my eye. That school provides me with one of the great joys of my life—a joy I would not know if my sense of gratitude were out of whack. The best part is that I know the children will remember how the school changed their lives, and that they in turn will change the lives of others.

The opportunity to make a difference in the lives of others does not thrust itself upon us, but we do not need to look hard for it, either. So when you spot the chance to give back to the world, act on it. You will have made life better. For others . . . and for yourself.

A GOLFER'S HEROES

I doubt you'll be surprised at the people I look up to. Other than a political leader whom I particularly revere, they are all among the elite of golf. However, you might be surprised at the reasons I hold them in such esteem.

SIR WINSTON CHURCHILL

Even though the great man wasn't much for golf, his bulldog persistence is the stuff that golfers need to get the most of out of their games. During the fallow years of his political career between the World Wars, Churchill was often ignored by the party in power in Britain, and a good many of British citizens thought he was a man who lived in the past—a symbol of the Victorian Age. When the second war became most dire, Churchill took the reins of freedom in the darkest hour. It is a cliché to say a man has iron will, but Churchill truly did. I find that when I need to dig deep within myself, it is helpful to think of Sir Winston's determination to see a job through to the end no matter what happens along the way.

JACK NICKLAUS

In the 1969 Ryder Cup, Jack Nicklaus was playing in the deciding match with an Englishman named Tony Jacklin. For the first time in years, the British team had a chance to win the competition. Of course, they had a chance to lose it as well. On the final hole of the match, Jacklin had a short putt that, if made, would cause the event to end in a tie, and if missed, would give victory to the Americans. The putt was of sufficient distance that under the pressure-filled circumstances, it could have easily been missed. With the weight of his entire nation upon his shoulders, Jacklin faced an unbearable strain. Realizing this, Nicklaus conceded the putt (as one can do in match play) and said to Jacklin, "I don't think you would have missed that putt, but I wasn't going to give you the opportunity to do so." If you ever want to explain to your children what it means to take the high road or what the definition of sportsmanship is, have them read this little story.

ARNOLD PALMER

There was a time in the late 1950s when the best American golfers were content to stay home and compete in America.

This was understandable when one considers that the largest amount of prize money was available in America and that travel in those days was no easy thing. However, the game had fans all over the world, and the game's oldest championship, the Open Championship in Scotland, was suffering from the lack of American participation. In fact, the grand old championship was in danger of becoming something of an anachronism because the absence of America's best players led to a decline in fan interest. Into this void stepped Arnold Palmer, he of the dashing good looks and daring style of play. When no other Americans saw fit to go to the Open in Scotland, Palmer went again and again and again. By example, Palmer showed American players on the rise the importance of the old championship. Moreover, he showed them what it meant to share their talent with those who loved the game.

BEN HOGAN

Many of you are probably familiar with the story of how Ben Hogan was nearly killed in an automobile accident and how doctors told him he might never walk again. Within a year,

Hogan was walking and playing and eventually winning the big championships. This is a wonderful tale of determination, but it is not why Ben Hogan should be someone you admire. The admirable thing about Hogan was his work ethic—his commitment to fulfilling his talent by looking for answers "in the dirt." Hogan was a talented player who struggled for many years before finding success, but during his early years he never once quit trying as hard as he could. Never, ever did Ben Hogan expect that the game, or success at it, would come easy to him. He embodies the idea that nothing worth achieving comes easily. For the very same reason, young Tiger Woods is a very admirable man. It is impossible to envy his success because he is so deserving of it.

BILLY CASPER

During the 1960s, Billy Casper was overshadowed by The Big Three in terms of recognition. His talent, however, was not eclipsed. Before his career on the PGA Tour came to its conclusion, he had won 51 events, placing him sixth on the all-time career victory list. On top of that, he won two U.S. Opens and the Masters Tournament. Billy Casper was an enormous talent, but the reason he is on this list is because he was a man who achieved balance in his life. His golf game was important to him, but he never lost sight of the fact that he was part of a bigger world. Over the years, he and his wife almost continually adopted children from all over the world in the hope of giving those kids a shot at a better life. That is worth more than every golf championship ever played.

LEE TREVINO

It would have been easy for Lee Trevino to be frightened by success. He grew up dirt poor in Texas and learned to play the game at a public driving range. While players like myself and Nicklaus and Palmer were spending our formative years as professional golfers playing every week, he was in the U.S. Marines. Trevino played golf in the Marines, but it was nothing that could prepare him for world-class competition. In the late 1960s, the perception of golf was still very much that of a blue-blood game, and the country club nature of the game still meant it was viewed as exclusionary. Into this

scene bounced the wise-cracking and seriously talented Mex-
ican-American named Lee Trevino. Not only was he unafraid
of the "golf world" but he was also unafraid of us—his competitors. That can only come from one place: the heart. Lee
Trevino had enough heart for 10 men. He eventually won two
U.S. Opens, two Open Championships, and two PGA Championships. The thing to be learned from him is that you cannot
let anything stand in the way of your dreams.

lesson five

Fear

WHY IT'S EASIER

TO FIGHT THAN TO RUN

It is the high summer of 1968, and I am in the small town of Carnoustie on the east coast of Scotland. I am competing for the game's oldest (first played in 1860) and most sought-after title, that of Open Champion. I have won the title before, back in 1959 at Muirfield, not very far from Carnoustie. It is the Saturday afternoon of the championship's final round (back in those days, the Open started on Wednesday and ended on Saturday), and as the tournament nears its conclusion, I am in position to grab the title and silver claret jug that goes to the winner.

Even though people are clamoring about, the scene allows me brief moments of reflection. Carnoustie is a stark place. With the North Sea churning away off to one side and the seemingly ancient gray town off to the other, Carnoustie is not the type of place that gives one cause to consider the wonders of life. Rather, it offers a smack of reality. As I walk along the final holes, it occurs to me that things have changed quite a bit since I won the Open Championship in 1959. The biggest change since those days is embodied by the man stalking the fairway alongside me: Jack Nicklaus. Even though this is only his 7th year as a professional, he is already considered one of the best-ever players. He is an intense and iron-willed competitor, which I admire. He is 28 and I am 33, and in that moment in time, those 5 years make a big difference. Competitively speaking, Nicklaus is still a man-cub—albeit a brilliant one!—and is relatively unscathed from battle. I, on the other hand, am a seasoned player and undeniably a man now. I have been in many more battles than Jack has, and since I do not possess his natural talent, I have had to fight like hell in every single one of them.

The amalgamation of age and experience is invaluable to a competitor; the self-awareness it imbues the player with is almost uncanny. Self-awareness, however, is accompanied by something to which young competitors (and young people in general) are completely oblivious: fear.

At this moment, I feel fear for the first time on the golf course. Mind you, I am not overwhelmed by fear, but it is present, and I know that uncontrollable fear starts out as a niggling worry like the one I have now. If Jack Nicklaus senses for one moment that I am wavering, he will crush me.

***

All triumphs in life are a complete test of skill *and* character. In order to win a championship or a personal victory of any type, you must subject yourself to the oddest of torments. As the pressure builds in any situation, it is normal to yearn for escape. This is fear in its most simple form—the feeling that

things would be made much easier by avoiding the
challenge that is about to transpire. The torment lies
in the tug of war between your instincts, which say
"Run!" and your spirit, which says, "Stand fast and
fight." Any decision to run is, of course, accompanied by the knowledge that you have given up and
that you can never go back to that moment. How
empty the spirit must be when reflecting upon such
moments.

The most significant common intangible
among the truly great is that they *enjoy adversity*.
They want to be put in fear-inducing situations because they know it is the ultimate test. The true
prize is not the trophy; rather, it is the knowledge
that at precisely the right moment, one is able to exercise absolute self-control and precise judgment.
This, in turn, allows the skills to take over, and the
triumph follows. In the afterglow of victory, the
best-remembered moments are those when the fear
was acknowledged and put to rest.

As that round at Carnoustie chugged along toward its zenith, I muttered to myself repeatedly, "I

must beat this guy. I know I can beat this guy." And when the moment was upon me—a fight-or-flight moment after Nicklaus struck a beautiful blow that had the crowd on its ear—I played one of the finest shots of my career, and it carried me to victory. The shot, a fairway wood to a green I could not see, ended up 2 feet from the hole. (In fact, in one of the more famous quotes of my career, I later told sportswriters that the ball "was flying on such a direct line toward the top of the flagstick that I had to lean sideways to see it.")

Take me back to that place right now and give me 1,000 golf balls, and I doubt I could hit one so pure or so close to the hole. To anyone watching that long-ago day, the shot I hit may have appeared effortless. The fact is, the pressure of the moment *was directly responsible for producing one of the best shots of my career*. And here is why: When you are under pressure and fearful, it becomes crystal clear to you that nothing but your absolute best will suffice. It actually lends clarity to the situation. Since you know that you truly need your best effort, you can clear your mind and allow your skills to trigger the act. As I stood on that fairway at Carnoustie, I said to myself, "You've been practicing your entire life to produce your best effort at moments such as this one. Trust your preparation, check your grip, check your stance, aim, and fire."

The beauty of this approach is that while you're actually simplifying things under pressure, those around you are typically magnifying the complexity of things. This is precisely what Rudyard Kipling meant when he wrote, "If you can keep your head when all about you [people] are losing theirs . . . " Do you recall the finish of that famous poem? It says, " . . . you'll be a man, my son."

If you seek success in any form, you are obliged to make your best effort in the face of adversity. The secret to achieving this best effort is clarity of thought and focus. Achieve this, and you will execute. Then, watch as the wall of fear crumbles down around you.

Winning

TAKING ADVANTAGE

OF LIFE'S OPPORTUNITIES

As one of the busiest and best competitors in the history of golf, I have played in somewhere around 2,000 professional tournaments. I have won more than 160 titles. You don't have to be a math whiz to realize that means that I have won fewer than 10 percent of the tournaments in which I have competed. These figures tell a story that is unique to championship golf: No matter how good you are, the first-place finishes are few and far between. In golf, the rarity of victories makes them more cherished and worthy of more dogged pursuit.

Some people would aver that the essence of competition can be found simply in taking part. I agree with that to a certain degree, but the truth is that all true competitors play to win. Victory should not come at all costs—a first-place finish achieved by duplicity, outright cheating, or poor sportsmanship is not a victory—but it must be the ultimate goal of the serious competitor.

This opinion may sound odd coming from a man who plays a game where losing is, statistically speaking, hundreds of times more common than winning. However, when you consider how difficult it is to win at golf, it becomes quite apparent that anything less than a total commitment to winning means that you will probably *never* come out on top. The same can be said for all pursuits.

First-place finishes are just as spare for the top amateur and club player as they are for professionals. The corollary between the game of golf and the pursuit of excellence in the rest of our lives is an obvious one, then, isn't it? The opportunities to achieve our goals are so rare that when they present themselves, we must give the fullest effort of which we are capable.

Over the decades of my career, I have been enjoined in battle with so many talented players who were equal to me in terms of the will to win—Arnold Palmer, Jack Nicklaus, Tom Watson, Lee Trevino, Seve Ballesteros—the list could go on for many more names. I won my share of those battles, and so did the other fellows. I'd like to share with you my state of mind when I find myself in position to win a golf tournament.

The first thing I do when I feel I have a chance to win is internally acknowledge what is transpiring. I actually have a little conversation with myself that goes something like this: "Things are coming down to the line, and you're right there in the fight. Nicklaus and Palmer are *not* going to give this thing to you. You have a chance, so you'd *better* get in there and do it, because who knows when you'll get another chance like this." Your mind is so extraordinary that it knows what is going on before you tell it, but a self-conversation like this one is your way of acknowledging that you are ready for the challenge.

I will say without hesitation that you cannot achieve any goal if you have negative thoughts running through your head. You must have positive and, what might seem to others, bold thoughts. This is not to say that you should ignore the strengths of an opponent, whether on the golf course, on a sales call, or in the boardroom. Acknowledge his strengths? Yes. Dwell on them? No.

In considering your opponent when it comes to crunch time, you should focus on his weaknesses and how your strengths can take advantage of those weaknesses. I have never played against any golfer who didn't have a weakness, and by focusing on those things, I have been able to convince myself at every turn that I am the better player in any given situation.

By the summer of 1965, I had won three of the four major championships in golf. The only one to elude me was the United States Open Championship. Over the four scheduled rounds of that event that year, I played well enough to get into an 18-hole playoff with a savvy veteran player named Kel Nagle. Kel was from Australia and was a very talented player. In 1960 he had thwarted Arnold Palmer's chances for the Grand Slam by pipping him at the Open Championship in St. Andrews, Scotland. The evening prior to our playoff, I searched my mind for a weakness in Kel's game. I couldn't find one. Then it occurred to me: Nagle was a much older fellow than I—a good 10 to 15 years, I figured. My advantage, it seemed to me, was my comparative physical youth.

I went directly to the weight room. Even though I weighed just 165 pounds, I clearly recall doing squats of 325 pounds that evening. Regardless of the great strength that I felt while doing this, it also made me feel young and full of physical vitality. In my mind, I knew Kel Nagle could not squat 325 pounds. The next day I was filled with confidence as a result. I won the playoff and the United States Open title—and the Grand Slam of golf.

In the heydays of The Big Three (which is

what the press called me, Arnold, and Jack), I had
to admit a few things to myself: Arnold and Jack
were bigger and stronger than I ever would be. But
I had a strength that neither had: I was physically
fit, and much more so than either of them. Over the
long haul of a tournament, I knew that my fitness
was just as much of an advantage over them as their
size and strength were over me. I was always aware
of our respective advantages, and as such, I never
once looked at Arnold or Jack and thought, "He's
better than me" or "He's going to beat me." The
truth is that in my mind, *I* was bigger and stronger
than they were. I've said that many times in my life,
and people tell me I'm a nut. But if using the power
of your mind to achieve your goals when you are
matched against the very best makes a person a nut,
so be it: I'm a nut.

No matter what situation you find yourself in,
you can win if you focus on and exploit, in your
own mind, the weaknesses of your opponent—
whatever they may be. Perhaps he's unprepared.

Maybe he's overconfident. Maybe, as in the case of
Kel Nagle and me, you simply have the calendar on
your side. See the weakness and use it as the foundation of your confidence. In these situations, trust
the power of your mind. If you can convince yourself that *now* is the moment to win, nothing can
stop you.

A GOLFER'S WORDS
OF INSPIRATION

Many profound thoughts have been said about the game of golf—enough to fill large volumes. Here are just a few that I find insightful, motivating, or merely amusing.

"Confidence, of course, is an admirable asset to a golfer, but it should be an unspoken confidence. It is perilous to put into speech. The gods of golf lie in wait to chasten the presumptuous."

—SIR P. G. WODEHOUSE,
author

"Most of us have a real warped idea of the amount of control we have over anything. It's not that we can't control certain aspects of this game, it's that we think we can control everything. That's where our error is. Then God says, 'Wait a minute, just so you don't forget.' A fleck of grass throws a putt off line, the ball is stuck in a tree or shoots this way and that. The elements, the variables, the unexpected. That's golf."

—ANNETTE THOMPSON,
professional golfer

"Have you learned lessons only from those who admired you, and were tender with you, and who stood aside for you? Have you not learned great lessons from those who rejected you, and braced themselves against you, or disputed the passage with you?"

—WALT WHITMAN,
poet

"There is no shape nor size of body, no awkwardness nor ungainliness, which puts good golf beyond reach. There are good golfers with spectacles, with one eye, with one leg, even with one arm. In golf, while there is life there is hope."

—SIR WALTER SIMPSON,
early–twentieth century golfer

"On the golf course, a man may be the dogged victim of inexorable fate, be struck down by an appalling stroke of tragedy, become the hero of unbelievable melodrama, or the clown in a side-splitting comedy."

—BOBBY JONES,
the finest amateur golfer of all time

A Golfer's Words of Inspiration

"The score is important, of course. And the discovery that you are superior to another golfer is satisfying. But when your score is bad and the other fellow beats you, golf still has been a blessing to you. The score isn't the be all and the end all."

—TOMMY ARMOUR,
winner of the 1931 Open Championship

"The force, the mass of character, mind, heart, or soul that a man can put into any work is the most important factor in that work."

—A. P. PEABODY
(I have no idea who this chap is, but I couldn't agree more with him. It applies nicely to golf.)

"What separates the great players from the good players or the 15-handicap player from the 20-handicap player is not so much ability as brainpower and emotional equilibrium."

—ARNOLD PALMER

"You learn golf all the time, but you don't learn it all at once."

—DAVIS LOVE JR.,
noted teaching professional and father
of PGA Tour player Davis Love III

"Go find some stimulating, fulfilling, challenging human endeavor that, unlike golf, does not require a commitment of time and effort to realize maximum enjoyment. And call me when you find it."

—JIM FLICK,
noted teaching professional and
swing coach to Jack Nicklaus

"This is my attitude toward my favorite game. I have its honor to support. So has each one who enters its fold. An error in count, an error that moves the ball, an error that in any way makes you take improper advantage over your opponent, seen or unseen, is the worst error in the whole game. We begin [each hole] with the question, 'Who has the honor?'

—GLENNA COLLETT VARE,
legendary female golfer
of the early twentieth century

A Golfer's Words of Inspiration

"The first thing you should do when you see that your ball has settled in a divot is to tell yourself that it's a bad break, that it happens to everyone, and that you really have to concentrate on this shot. You might also resolve to never leave a divot unrepaired yourself."

—KEN VENTURI,
1964 U.S. Open Champion
and golf analyst for CBS Sports

"The man who can go into a patch of rough alone, with the knowledge that only God is watching him, and play his ball where it lies is the man who will serve you faithfully and well."

—SIR P. G. WODEHOUSE,
author

"The harder you practice the luckier you get."

*—This is a quote from me, actually.
One of my more famous utterances and
one that proves true to this day.
It was first said in response
to a gallery member who opined
that I had hit a lucky shot.*

"Dare to be wise; begin! He who postpones the hour of living rightly is like the rustic who waits for the river to run out before he crosses."

—HORACE,
Roman poet before the birth of Christ.
(What he's telling you is that you cannot get there if you do not start.)

"I find that a great part of the information I have was acquired by looking up something and finding something else along the way."

—FRANKLIN P. ADAMS,
writer
Learning begets learning. This doesn't apply just to books, either. Think of what you learn in life by doing something you haven't done before.

"There is no type of miracle that cannot happen at least once in golf."

—GRANTLAND RICE,
legendary sportswriter

"The trouble with all of us, who grumble over the game and thus spoil an otherwise pleasant afternoon with congenial

friends, is that we do not understand the game, nor ourselves. In this we can take a number of lessons from the poorer player who without fail has fun. For no matter how good we may be, if we should fancy that we have mastered golf to the extent that we can go out day after day and play as we please, then we are greater fools than ought to be left at large."

—BOBBY JONES,
amateur golf great

Dignity and Honor

**HOW THE GAME WILL IMBUE YOU WITH
THE MOST ELUSIVE HUMAN QUALITIES**

A lesson that competitive golf has taught me—a few too many times, I must admit—is that a person's dignity and honor always get tested at times when we really wish they wouldn't. This is precisely the reason why maintaining a sense of honor can be so challenging. Everything is going along as well as could be hoped for and then—whammo!—adversity strikes. But what a sweet victory it is when in such times, you handle yourself in a way you will never regret.

Years ago, I was playing in a tournament in Greensboro, North Carolina. We had to play the final two rounds in a single day, and after a morning round in which I shot 67, I was in good position to win the tournament. Prior to starting the morning round, we had been informed that we would have 14 minutes for lunch between rounds.

In those days, a player signed his scorecard after a round while sitting in a small tent with the fellows he played with while a volunteer offered us soft drinks. (In comparison, today we sign our scorecards in larger tents with tournament officials standing by to make sure no mistakes are made.) Upon entering the tent to sign my scorecard, I was greeted by a young woman as she offered me some orange juice and said, "You have 15 minutes for lunch, Mr. Player."

"No," I said, "we have 14 minutes."

"It's been adjusted to 15 minutes," she said.

Either way, it made little difference, but the conversation distracted me, and I left the tent without signing my scorecard. When I realized what I had done, I went back into the tent and signed my card. By the time I got to the first tee to begin the final round, I realized that what I had done—exiting the scoring area and then re-entering to sign my scorecard—may have been a violation of the rules. I saw a tournament official named Jack Tuthill standing nearby, and I told him what had occurred.

"Gary," said Mr. Tuthill, "your instincts are correct. That is a rules violation. I hate to tell you this, but you're disqualified."

At the time, I was leading the tournament by five shots over Arnold Palmer. That didn't matter. I packed my bags and headed down the road. And you know what? I did not feel at all bad about what happened. I felt a little silly, perhaps, because I had let myself get distracted. I know, too, that I could have very easily played that round and won the tournament without anyone being the wiser. To do so would have been as simple as keeping my mouth shut. But what a hollow victory that would have been, if I could not say to myself that I had not done everything on the up and up.

As you have read, I want to win as badly as

anyone who ever played the game. But to do so at the cost of my own honor and the honor of the game—well, the very idea of it is an anathema to me. Since the Rules of Golf call for self-policing, we as golfers frequently encounter moments when the right thing to do is to call a penalty on ourselves. The only thing you can do to prepare for such moments in life is to vow to yourself that when they arise, you will know the right thing to do and that you will, without hesitation, do it.

I am sure there are those who think that what I did at that tournament years ago was ridiculous. My infraction was technical and trivial, completely unrelated to my on-the-course performance. But here's the thing: If I had not turned myself in, I would have had to live the rest of my life with the knowledge that I had cheated. And the money and prestige of one tournament certainly aren't worth that. Much better is the feeling I have today that even though I left a trophy and check behind— money that would be long gone by now—I still have my dignity and honor.

Why have things changed so much?

On the current-day sporting scene, it is not at all uncommon to see and hear the great majority of athletes display a lack of respect for their opponents both as human beings and fellow competitors. As for the lack of dignity with which they treat themselves, it leaves me almost speechless. The idea of humility is lost on all but a handful of modern sportsmen, and the lack of it is visible in the ludicrous antics we see when an athlete does no more than the task he is paid to do (such as score a basket or make a first down) and then acts as if he had single-handedly stormed Omaha Beach. To be blunt, it's disgraceful. It gives me a tremendous feeling to see that, win or lose, Tiger Woods always removes his cap before shaking hands with his fellow competitors at the completion of play. It is a small thing, but it matters a great deal. It is a matter of dignity.

I have heard it said many times of my good friend Jack Nicklaus that he is never more admirable than he is in defeat. Jack never made any bones about the fact that he wanted to beat your brains out on the golf course, but when he came out on the short end of the fight, he unfailingly conducted himself with grace and honor. Jack learned this quality from his father, Charlie, who told Jack as a young boy that when things didn't go his way, he should look the other fellow directly in the eye, shake his hand, say "congratulations"—*and mean it*. In this regard, Jack has been a model for both his contemporaries, such as myself, and the players who have come after him. His awareness of his own dignity and that of others is monumental and worth emulating at any level.

The game of golf provides us with a never-ending stream of challenges to our honor and dignity. The insights these challenges offer into our own souls provide us with an invaluable commodity—the ability to look at ourselves in the mirror and know we are honorable men. To attempt to define honor is a difficult task. In my mind I have always thought of it as doing the right thing, when to do the wrong thing is a much easier and seemingly beneficial choice. At its highest level, honor is personified by men who die on the field of battle fighting for a just cause. It would be easier and certainly more beneficial to run, but they stand. That is honor. Thankfully, most of us never face such a choice in life, but we are presented with many smaller opportunities to prove to ourselves that we do possess these admirable qualities (even if they are hard to pinpoint).

I have been in enough pitched battles on the golf course to be intimately familiar with the wildest possible emotional swings. In those moments, when you put everything you have into winning and it's not enough, it can be very difficult to maintain a proper level of respect for yourself and your opponents. But when you succeed in acting with heartfelt honor at such times, you have achieved a victory of even greater long-term value.

Physical Fitness

THE WAYS YOUR BODY

WILL REWARD YOU

Even though I was a gung ho participant in athletics from a very early age, the realization that I needed to relentlessly pursue a daily exercise program did not hit home until I played in my first Masters Tournament in 1957.

In those days, it was still a challenge to most players in the field to reach the greens of Augusta National's legendary par-fives in two shots. (Today, modern equipment and better-trained players have rendered this challenge nonexistent.) Personally, I could not reach *any* of the par-fives at Augusta in two shots. I noted, however, that the two best

American players, Arnold Palmer and Jack Nicklaus, could reach them with relative ease.

Upon seeing this, I knew that if I was ever going to match these fellows shot-for-shot, I would have to gain strength. That meant working out with weights at a time when it was considered foolish for a golfer to do so. The prevailing logic was that a muscle-bound golfer would lose the natural flexibility that allowed him to swing the club. I was convinced this was hogwash, and that by combining weight training and other exercises with the endless practice on my golf game, I could become stronger while maintaining the flexibility necessary to play championship golf. To say that people thought I was crackers would be to put it mildly, but I proved them wrong.

More than 40 years later, I continue to have a daily exercise routine. And I credit much of my success to it, both for the obvious reasons (being fit and limber did indeed help me lengthen my shots and win tournaments) and for some less than obvious reasons.

Here's what I mean. We are all born with some amount of determination. But often, we need more than what comes naturally to us. The additional determination we need to excel must be cultivated from within. After all these years, I have no doubt that this process of cultivation begins with the discipline of keeping our bodies in shape.

Staying fit requires time, dedication, and focus. Because it is such a challenge, fitness makes demands on our minds as well as our bodies. This in turn strengthens us mentally. In other words, I believe that conditioning the body conditions the mind at the same time and gives us the ability to be in control under pressure.

An example of this occurs when we stand on a tee box. There are two things you can think about in such situations: You can see the trouble and think, "I'd better not hit it there," or you can see the fairway and think, "I will hit it there." If you have prepared your body for the situation, your mind will impose its will on your body and say, "You will hit it in the fairway." If that sounds oversimplified to you, I can assure you it is not. It is the power of positive thinking.

The truth, friend, is that with all of the handy excuses and conveniences of the modern world, one of the greatest challenges we face is staying physically fit. If you accept this challenge, you will find that when other challenges come along, you can use your dedication to fitness as an example to yourself that you can do anything. You will be able to go into any situation with the belief that you are fully capable of achieving your goal. And you will never face a situation where you say, "I cannot do that."

I am surprised at how few people understand this. One of the responsibilities of a professional golfer is to compete in pro-am events the week of any tournament (except the major championships). In these events, weekend golfers get an opportunity to play with touring pros, and we touring pros get a chance to meet the golf fans who make our livelihoods possible. Many of the amateur partners I've had over the years are highly successful businessmen who have achieved their success with the same sort of mental determination that I have employed in my own career—which is why I am always amazed to see that many of them pay little attention to staying physically fit.

I am fully aware of the time constrictions people face in attempting to accomplish so much in the modern world, but I cannot empathize with people who say they have no time to exercise their bodies. If they only knew the added enjoyment they would get out of their business and personal lives if they committed an hour a day to staying fit—not to mention the mental benefits I've described—they would do so, starting today. To those who say, "I do not have the time," I say, "Make the time."

Today, my daily fitness routine lasts for 1 hour. When I am at home, it is the first thing I do, and I relish the opportunity to begin each day by working out. When I am on the tournament trail, my daily workout comes at the end of the day.

Trust me when I say that there are many

evenings when this is an immensely difficult task. After a day of playing and practicing, talking with the press, signing autographs, and attending the various functions I have a responsibility to be at, it would be much easier for me to say, "Maybe I'll skip my workout." But I never have—not even once. Experience has taught me that going through with a full workout at times when I do not feel like it does more than just tune my body. It also feeds the fierce self-discipline I need to sustain me when I am under pressure in tournaments.

Here's an example of a 1-hour workout I do:

- 30 minutes on a stationary bike.
- 300 crunches sprinkled throughout the hour. I do them in varying sets (i.e., I'll do 50 and then maybe I'll do 100) so my body doesn't get accustomed to a standard routine.
- What I call wrist rolls. This is a four-pound weight tied to a handle with rope. I roll the weight up and then slowly lower it. This strengthens my wrists and forearms.

- Three sets of one-legged squats. Weights as necessary.
- Various types of lower-back stretching because the golf swing is very hard on the lower back.
- 100 slow, right-handed swings with a very heavy-weighted club, then 100 left-handed swings (to balance my back muscles and build flexibility).

In those moments when I am alone in a hotel and do not feel like doing my workout, I am always grateful when I am finished. Once begun, the time flies by, and I am able to go to sleep knowing I did everything I could that day to keep my potential limitless.

THE SOUNDS OF GOLF

The sounds of golf are unique and sweet. Add to them the smell of the cut grass, the feel of the sun on your back, the sight of a distant flag waving, and you can't help but be transported to a better place. Here are some of the sounds that I particularly relish.

THE CLICK OF PERSIMMON

When woods were actually made of wood, there was nothing that could compare to the sound (a combined "click" and "swoosh") and feel of a golf ball smashing against persimmon wood. It was soft and hard at the same time. Beautiful and violent. Today you hit a golf ball, and it sounds like you dropped a bucket. My suggestion is to keep a persimmon driver around—buy one at a garage sale if you have to—and when you're feeling stressed, go to the driving range and hit a few balls with it. The persimmon click is the symphony of golf.

THE CRUNCH
OF STEEL SPIKES ON CONCRETE

Whenever I am wearing my golf shoes and I walk across a paved surface, I am somehow reassured by the crunching noise I hear. It's the audio version of comfort food. When I hear the crunch, I know I'm in the right place, among the right people, doing something I love.

WHITE NOISE

Sometimes on the treeless links alongside the ocean in Scotland, Ireland, and England, the wind can rip so fiercely by the ears that it leaves one unable to hear any other sound. It creates a sense of isolation—even if your mates are just a few feet away—that somehow makes a person keenly aware of the simplicity of their existence. The complexities we create for ourselves in life are carted off on the wind, and we see ourselves at the most base level. It is not just a figure of speech: The white noise and fresh ocean air literally cleanse our minds.

THE SILENT SOUNDS OF MORNING

Having the opportunity to be the first group off the tee on any given day gives a golfer the opportunity to experience sensations that otherwise would be lost in the noise of midday. The mornings are silent. The players are less apt to be chatty, and cool air and dewy ground are conducive to sticking hands in pockets and walking noiselessly along. Only in the morning do you hear the sound created by shoe bottoms grazing the tops of the grass. Only in the morning does the sound of irons clinking together in the golf bags reverberate through the trees and seem to carry for miles. Only in the morning do you hear your ball land on the green 150 yards away, making a thud like it would if you dropped it on the ground next to you. These seldom-heard sounds help us appreciate the solitary nature of our game.

THE MUSIC OF DUSK

The early evening also is a magic time on golf courses. The number of players on the course is thinning out. The natural light is at its richest, and the colors surrounding us take on their most brilliant hues. Shadows creep across the landscape, giving definition to humps and hollows. And just when you think it can't get any better, nature's orchestra comes to life: crickets and bullfrogs and tree frogs and assorted other musicians. These sounds remind us that we share our game with nature—and that we should be respectful of that fact.

LAUGHTER

There is no other sport that gives us so many opportunities to laugh with our friends. The game can be so absurd at times that laughter is the only thing that keeps us from going insane. One of the finest sounds in golf is encountered when we enter the grillroom after a round. What we inevitably hear is the sound of men laughing together at the foibles of the round just ended. The laughter reminds us that no matter how solitary our pursuit, we are never truly alone in our frustration.

THE PUFF OF THE SAND

When a ball goes in the sand, the sound we want to hear on our escape shot is very distinct. If we don't hit enough sand and catch all ball, what we hear is the crack of the club against ball. That's an ugly sound. If we hit too much sand, we hear a sound similar to that of a shovel being driven into the sod. That's an ugly sound as well. On the perfect sand shot, we hear a soft puff as the club slides through the sand just beneath the ball. That is a beautiful sound.

THE RATTLE OF THE FLAGSTICK

All of us have hit horrible shots only to look up in wonder as our ball—screaming out of control and moving much too fast—collides with the flagstick and drops down next to or into the hole. It's a jarring sound—the rattle of fiberglass lingering in the air for a few seconds. In those few seconds, however, we realize that that rattle is the sound of reprieve. For no obvious reason, we have been granted new life on a hole.

Sportsmanship

THE ENJOYABLE

COEXISTENCE OF LIFE

Once every 2 years, a small team of the best professional golfers from the United States competes against a similar team of players from Europe. At stake is a small trophy called the Ryder Cup.

The event was founded with the intention that it would bring together brother professionals in the spirit of good sportsmanship. But over the last decade, it has digressed into something more comparable to a schoolyard fracas, replete with utter nonsense—such as some players saying they do not like certain individuals on the opposing team. Some simpletons have even chosen to describe it as a war.

The verbal rubbish surrounding the event has had a disastrous effect on the behavior of golf fans both in America and in Europe. Both sides—players and fans—have displayed equal amounts of boorishness. As a player who plays on both continents and as one who was never eligible to play in the event because I'm neither American nor European, I can make these statements in an honest and unbiased manner. The reason I make them is because I cannot bear the thought that petty jingoism might bring down a game with a tradition that depends heavily upon the mutual respect among players.

I will go so far as to say that the current-day Ryder Cup does not offer a good example for young people to follow. A young person who is just starting out in golf should not be forced to associate that kind of garbage with a sport that is otherwise above reproach.

To think that you cannot be highly competitive and be friends with your opponents is just baloney. At the very least, two people competing for anything owe each other respect. I'm not foolish enough to think that every person will become thick friends with every individual he meets in life. We are all too diverse for that to happen. It is very possible, however, to understand that when you vie with someone for the same objective, he is doing the same thing you are: trying his best to achieve a personal goal. If that makes him a bad person, what does it make you?

The true value of sportsmanship does not lie solely in the fact that it is always an admirable idea to take the high road. As you well know by now, I think winning is important—very important. But winning is not the only thing. There have never been three golfers in the history of the game who simultaneously compiled the championship records that Jack Nicklaus, Arnold Palmer, and I have. Nor have there ever been three players who wanted to win so badly. Through all that, the three of us have maintained mutual respect and have become friends. In fact, we are friends enough that we have spent time at each other's homes and have gone on holiday together. Those were richly rewarding times

for us emotionally, and they never would have occurred without the respect we had for each other.

It is easy to see why it is that people all too
readily fall into the notion that someone else might
be "the enemy." The very fact that they seek the
same goal as us means that they seek to vanquish
our hopes and dreams. Rather than revile someone
for this, you should understand that it serves to
make your own accomplishments—whatever they
may be—all the sweeter. When you triumph, you
will have overcome the very best effort that your
opponent had to offer, and you will more than
likely find that you raised your own level of performance beyond a level of capability you ever dreamed
possible. And if you are defeated—as we all are at
some point—there is no shame as long as you
brought your full effort to the tussle. Such moments
provide you with an opportunity to see an often
hidden side of yourself. To paraphrase a verse from
Proverbs, when you enjoy the success of others, you
guarantee that there will be those who enjoy your
own successes when they come.

There are many stories about how during World War I, the troops from both sides would cease hostilities during Christmastime and, in some cases, even get together and sing in shared moments of humanity. These were men who were literally trying to kill each other, and yet they were still able to look out across No-Man's-Land and realize that on the other side there was a group of men who were in the same situation.

There is a tendency among people to think that the other guy doesn't understand our lives, that he can't possibly know what something means to us or how hard we've tried. In truth, he knows all those things because he is living them himself. That is why he deserves your respect and even appreciation for his efforts.

We are all very different people, even those of us who appear to be much the same. There is no such thing as a typical American, a typical Englishman, or a typical South African. To know this is to become a part of something quite special, a part of humanity that revels in the notion that we are all just one amidst an ocean of superb individuals. Rest assured, there is nothing in the world like the feeling you get when you triumph and know that all those you have beaten look upon you with respect and admiration, and that they know you feel the same way on their big days. You will enjoy these moments often in life—as long as you never forget that respect is a two-way street.

lesson ten

Exploring

SEEKING OUT

CHALLENGES

From the earliest days of my professional career, I knew I was going to have to travel a considerable amount if I wanted my career to amount to anything. In the first place, I wouldn't have made much of a living as a professional golfer if I had stayed put in South Africa. More important, however, I wouldn't have proven much to myself or anyone else if I didn't travel abroad and play against the best players in the world.

All of the greatest players in history have made it a point to go to lands that are foreign to them in order to fully test their mettle. Once I started traveling in search of challenges, I was hooked. To date, I have traveled somewhere in the neighborhood of 12 million miles to compete in tournaments and design golf courses. Along the way, I have received an education that is only available to those who have the explorer's spirit within them.

Strictly in a golf sense, my travels have taught me that until you exhaust your study of a subject, you never fully comprehend it. If you don't fully comprehend something, you cannot get the maximum amount of joy out of it. The golf I played in South Africa as a young man was similar to the type of golf played in the United States. By that I mean it was a target game where a player focuses almost exclusively on moving the ball from point to point through the air, safe in the knowledge that the ball will not run very far along the ground. Since it was possible to gauge almost precisely how the ball would react once it hit the ground, I was able to play the game feeling as if I were in control at almost every point.

Some of my earliest travels took me all the

way up to England and Scotland, the latter being the country where the game has its roots. Had I never made those trips, I would never have known that the game existed on an entirely different plane than that with which I was accustomed. On the rolling, windswept, seaside links of Britain, I learned that golf could be wildly unpredictable and that even the best players had only a minimal amount of control over what happened to a given shot. If there was an absence of rain, the ground could become as hard as an airport runway, and the ball could skitter along the ground to who knew where. This meant I had to learn a whole new side of the game. I had to learn to play shots that stayed close to the ground and bounded along toward their destination.

There were two reasons for this: The wind on the seaside links used for the Open Championship in Scotland often howled so fiercely that the higher a ball was hit into the air, the more peril it faced. A low shot could be played with more "sting" to it, and the lower trajectory exposed it to less buffeting by the wind. Second, the ball had to run up to the hole because if it landed on the green it would bounce into rough. And believe me when I tell you that the word "rough" is very accurate in describing the long fescue and gnarled grasses that surround the playing areas on links courses. What a challenge this "new" type of golf presented to me! I knew that all of the game's greats had conquered this style of golf and that if I was to be counted among them, so must I.

The end result of my early travels to the United Kingdom was that I learned to appreciate a side of something that had previously been unknown to me. In a larger sense, my travels have revealed the wonders of the world and its people to me. I am convinced that frequent traveling is the single finest education a person can attain.

By nature, most people are somewhat suspicious of the people "on the other side of the hill" from them. By this I mean that if we are not familiar with something, we allow it to frighten us to varying degrees. Yet we also have endless admiration for explorers and adventurers. The reason for the latter point is that we see something good in their lack of fear and also in their insatiably curious minds. There is nothing standing in the way of your becoming one of the admired people in this sense. Even if you don't have the financial wherewithal to travel the globe, I'll bet there are places just a few miles from where you live that you've never taken the time to explore. Take a long walk or get in the car and go spend a weekend somewhere you've never been before, even if you don't know what is there. At the very least, you will add to your life experience, and you might even discover something magnificent.

I am often struck by the insularity people wrap themselves in, and I wonder what people are thinking when they refuse the opportunity to travel. Today in South Africa, there is a professional golf tournament, which I founded, worth $2 million to the winner, and there are only 12 invited players in the field. It is played at the Gary Player Country Club, and I am proud of the event's achievements over the last 20 years. I often ask some of the younger players I meet if they'd like to play in it, and they offer up excuses for not making the trip. They are "tired" or "burned out" or they have a luncheon date with their Granny that week. These excuses nauseate me. It would kill me not to accept that challenge if it were offered to me. I'd get in a bloody rowboat and cross the Atlantic if that's what I needed to do. What perturbs me about these attitudes is that those who decline don't realize how lucky they are to be offered such an opportunity. To borrow a notion from Mark Twain, in 20 years you won't be so bothered by what you did; rather, you'll be bothered by what you didn't do. The intellectual and emotional rewards of exploring life are waiting for you around the corner and across the seas. Go and get them.

THE TRANSCENDENT
MOMENTS OF A GOLFER

Ask any amateur golfer what the game is like, and it won't take long before you start to hear the challenges and frustrations. Golf is a decidedly hard and merciless game. So what keeps us coming back? The simple pleasures of playing, certainly. But also, the potential that on any shot, something amazing will happen. Here are some of the moments I most cherish on the course.

PLAYING GOLF AT LAND'S END

Every time I have the opportunity to play a golf course that borders an ocean, I am overcome with excitement. For starters, I know the challenge of the game will be on the high end of the scale because of the wind. Beyond that, however, I know that my companion for the day is going to be the sea and all the wonder that goes with it: the tempo of the surf pounding against the shore, the smell, and most of all the feeling of awe that accompanies simply looking out over the ocean. The quiet power of nature is never more apparent than when we look at the unrelenting movement of the sea. It is so mysterious: What is out there? Where has it been? Where is it going? I feel that playing along the ocean presents us with a state of grace that we seldom feel in life. The wonders of the sea keep our minds sharp and somehow seem to sharpen all of our other senses as well. Our steps quicken under us as we bound along the soft grasses, and the light seems to give things their richest possible hues. I cannot fully explain it, but if any game can make a man feel closer to God, it is the game of golf when played along the sea.

THE PURELY STRUCK SHOT

There is an expression in golf we use when we strike a shot exactly the way we want. We say, "I pured that one." These are the favorite words of any golfer because they are accompanied by the sweetest feeling a golfer can experience: the nerve-tingling rush of sensation that runs up the shaft of the club into our hands and arms and then disperses to every point of our bodies right down to our toes and up to our minds. These are the goose-bump shots in golf, the ones that feel so good because, in fact, we can barely feel them. The purity of the feeling lies in its subtlety and the speed that it is transmitted through our bodies. Why, we wonder, can't they all feel like that? Because in that moment, you have achieved perfection in an imperfect game. If they all felt like that, we wouldn't know how good the good ones feel.

THE HOLE-IN-ONE

We play the game a lifetime trying to achieve the lowest score. If we play with any level of competency and play long enough, chances are that eventually we will strike a shot on the tee of a par-three that ends up in the hole. Sometimes it is a wonderfully struck ball that covers the flag the entire way, and other times it is a ball that bounces off a hillside or ricochets off a tree and trundles across the green and into the hole. The beauty of these shots is that they lie beyond our ability to control things and really our ability to understand all things that happen. They make us realize that sometimes good things happen for reasons we cannot fathom and that this very feeling is part of the wonder of life. Since we cannot make everything happen in life, sometimes we just have to try our best and let happen what will.

GOING HOME AGAIN

We all have a favorite golf course. Perhaps it's the one we caddied on as children or the one we learned to play on. Maybe it's the golf course where we broke 100 or 90 or 80 for the first time. The fact that we accomplished something there, whether it was the understanding of human nature as a caddie or the realization of our own potential as players, imbues the place with a special feeling known only to us. In our constant search for new challenges, we travel around to play the game as often as circumstances allow. To return to our one place — "our course" — where we feel secure and familiar with each little bump in the ground and every limb on every tree, is to journey back to a place from which we can look upon all we have done in life. We can see clearly how far we have gone and how far we have yet to go. We see old friends, tell old stories, and wrap ourselves in the warmth of familiarity. It is the golfer's version of coming home from battle.

THE PICK-UP GAME

Any golfer worth his spikes has at times been overcome with the feeling that no matter what else needs to be done, he

must head out to the golf course and play right now. There is
no time to call friends and arrange a game because they will
be too busy. There is no time to hesitate because we do not
want the feeling to pass. So we head to the golf course, and
we wander down to the golf shop or the first tee and ask if
anyone could use a player to round out their group. There is
always a spot for us, and it is a spot among kindred spirits
just met. The worthwhile thing about such moments is that it
gives us the opportunity to get to know people we otherwise
would never meet. This is not to say that we will become fast
mates with the people we play a pick-up game with, but it is
to say that one of the great joys of the game is the possibility
that we may begin a round with a stranger and end it with a
new friend.

NEW LIFE

It is an intensely enlightening thing to be the first one to arrive at a golf course in the morning and watch the place come
to life. Upon arrival, the place is quiet, and you can look out
over the course as it beckons you to challenge yourself. Soon,

others arrive. The greens-keeping staff arrives and heads out onto the course to sweep the dew from the greens and cut the grass. The smell of the freshly mown grass carries on the wind, and what a glorious smell it is. The people who work in the golf shop arrive—the young assistant professionals, the caddiemaster, the caddies, the young men who work in the bag room—to begin anew the pursuit of the game and all of its moments. The other players trickle in and soon the place is a beehive of activity: the clanging of clubs together as bags are moved about, the click of practice balls being struck on the range, the voices of comradeship as players needle each other, make bets, inquire about how the most recent trip to Florida or Scotland or Scottsdale went. All of this in preparation for the moment when we begin the pursuit of our passion in the company of like-minded souls. Every round of golf is an opportunity to start all over again. What more could we ask?

Family

ACHIEVING BALANCE

IN YOUR LIFE

A professional golfer spends almost all of his day practicing at the golf course. And when it is time to compete, the professional golfer does all of his work on the road, usually with extended periods away from home. You can see how it might create problems on the home front.

In your own passionate pursuit of golf, you encounter the same problem on a smaller scale. By the time you travel to the golf course, warm up, play your round, chat with your mates a bit, and head home, you've used up a large part of the day. When you have a family that depends on you to share your life with them, the time you "steal" out of a day to play golf can make you feel plenty guilty.

I've learned over the years, however, that it doesn't have to be that way. Your pursuit of golf (or a career) does not have to come at the expense of time with your family. In fact, your golf game (or your work life) and a happy home life can be mutually beneficial.

The large amount of time I spend away from home has actually caused better communication between family members when I am at home. Because our time together as an entire family is precious—especially now that our children are grown and my wife, Vivienne, often travels with me—it is essential that we make the best possible use of that time. If we communicated poorly, we would be wasting that time.

One of the ways we avoid poor communication is by having what in Africa we call *indabas*. These are gatherings in which everyone is free to air any concerns or feelings they have on any subject. Since directness is the entire point of the exercise, everyone knows going into it that there is no point getting upset by the conversation. You tell me what it is that I do that's bothering you, and I will tell you what's on my mind. The end goal is for all parties involved to walk away knowing exactly what they must do to improve the quality of the relationship with each person. I also have *indabas* with the people who work with me, whether they are corporate workers in our offices in America, Europe, or Asia, or farm workers on my ranch in South Africa. These conversations can be intense at times, but they are incalculably valuable to those who participate in them.

Indabas are an old African custom, and quite a good one, too. They teach us the meaning behind what Sir Winston Churchill meant when he said, "Trust instinct to the end though it render no reason." If your instincts are telling you to talk about something with your wife or children, do it without hesitation. You might find that whatever you were concerned about was a figment of your imagination. There is an equal chance, however, that you'll discover that it had been on the minds of those you love as well. Since these conversations can be very emotional, we long ago decided that we would always end them with a prayer asking for the ability to carry through on whatever we had pledged to do during the discussion.

With frequent family *indabas*, I have come to realize that there is much truth in the old adage that it's not the quantity of the time spent with those we love that matters, but rather the quality. (By the way, it's not a bad idea to have mini-*indabas* with just your spouse whenever the need arises. Vivienne and I have a standing rule: If I do something you don't like, tell me immediately. I will do the same with you.) When I am able to be at something important, like one of our grandchildren's school plays or debate matches, I make certain I let them know how much I enjoyed it, and I make a big fuss in doing so. I always end by telling them how much I love them. I do the same with our own children, even though they are fully grown. The day you lose the ability to tell your children you love them—no matter how old they are—is the day you've lost something you cannot replace.

It is vitally important in life that we pursue our

goals with the clearest of minds. By regularly making certain the lines of communication are open along every channel, I am able to pursue my competitive dreams without the constant nagging feeling that I might somehow be leaving a family member in the lurch. The hidden blessing in all of this is that since I know I must be vigilant about keeping those lines of communication open, it provides me with a break from golf. This helps keep the sport a healthy and passionate pursuit for me rather than letting it become an unhealthy obsession.

As it turns out, the healthiest possible balance between passions and family occurs when the two become interdependent. Your passion pursued to its fullest is an even greater joy if you charge after it knowing your family is happy that you are doing what you love. They cannot give you that support if you don't live up to your end of the bargain when the time comes, however. In turn, you'll find greater success with the freedom of mind that comes with knowing you have fulfilled your obligations to your family's emotional needs.

Motivation

KEEPING YOUR

BATTERIES CHARGED

By the time I reached my late 30s, I was beginning to have doubts about whether I wanted to continue playing golf. I had experienced success in every possible way, both financially and emotionally. The bulk of my adult years had been spent almost solely in the pursuit of golf excellence. Success at this pursuit had given me a sense of purpose and accomplishment.

But around the time of the 1973 Open Championship at Troon in Scotland, I felt as if I had reached a moment in life where it might be time to move on from golf. I was 38 years old. During the subsequent months, I underwent surgery for a blocked urethra and tried to rush too quickly back to playing. This simply compounded the gloomy state of mind I was in.

At one point I said to my wife, Vivienne, "I feel like retiring. Let's go home and raise horses and do the things that maybe we've been missing out on." Her words were those of the most loving and concerned kind of partner: "Whatever you decide, it is your decision alone. I will support your decision no matter what." I admit that it would have been quite easy to quit if she had said, "Good idea. Let's go home for good."

The thing that kept gnawing at my psyche, however, was that if I did indeed quit, I would be doing so not because I truly wanted to raise racehorses and spend the rest of my life on our ranch. The truth was that I would be quitting because I felt I couldn't hack it anymore, that I could no longer compete with all the talented young men who were then emerging in the game.

At this critical moment in my life—some

might refer to it as a mid-life crisis—I thought back to my youth and about the things that the game of golf had taught me over the years. Reflecting on my boyhood days, I remembered rising at 5:00 A.M. to get on a streetcar in Johannesburg by 6:00 A.M. After getting off the streetcar, I'd walk across town a bit and then get on the Number 68 bus, a double-decker type, which would drop me off near school. By the time I got home at night, it was dark, and I often had to prepare my own supper. My mother had passed on and my father was still working. For lack of a less dramatic term, there had been a lot of sacrifices made to get me where I was, both on my own part and the part of my parents. What sort of man would I be to simply shrug off those years of struggle as unimportant and to quit simply because I felt like it?

As I had done so many times before in life, I looked to the game itself to provide me with motivation. There is motivation in every shot we play in golf. If the shot is played poorly, we instinctively think, "I must play that shot better the next time."

And even when we hit the shot exactly as we want, we think, "I can hit that shot even better the next time." Then I thought about what a thrill and privilege it had been for me to be locked in competition against the great players like Jack Nicklaus, Arnold Palmer, Lee Trevino, and Tom Watson. Never in my life had I felt more alive than when battling it out at close quarters with these men.

I even thought about how Vivienne liked to tease me about how she had once made two holes-in-one in the same round. I realized it was something I would probably never accomplish, but it nevertheless served to remind me that I had not done everything there was to do in golf.

We all arrive at points in life where we look around us and think, "Is this all there is? This is it? After all these years, here I am the same as I ever was?" Experience has taught me that these moments are to be expected, and when they come, we must meet them head on and say to ourselves, "Don't be such a fool. Do not just pass time on this Earth, *live* your life." The sorriest man is the man who knows he gave up before he exhausted his efforts because he must look back and wonder, "What if?"

If you stay determined to live life fully, you will never become a "what if" man; you'll be surprised by the sources of motivation that suddenly appear to you. During those moments for me in 1973, I happened upon the practice tee at a golf tournament where the sweet-swinging Irishman Christy O'Connor was working on his game. Christy swung the club with an effortless, sing-song motion that was unparalleled in golf (with the exception of Sam Snead). I had always been an aggressive swinger of the club. Here was the motivation I needed. I did not need to change my swing, but I was motivated by the potential for improvement if I did. I watched Christy intently for some time and then used the oldest trick in the golfer's book: If you think you are swinging like someone, you do swing like them (or at least it feels like you do). I went home to South Africa and worked on "being" Christy O'Connor. Suddenly things started looking up. I was striking the ball with my usual positive mindset and as a result, I became motivated to prove once again that I was one of the world's best golfers. I even said to my father one evening, "I'm not finished yet, Dad. I'll be back on top."

The next year, in 1974, I won the Masters Tournament, the British Open Championship, and seven other events around the world. I had taken one of the lowest points of my career and turned it into a triumph. We are all capable of doing such things when we acknowledge that we have never achieved all there is to do in our lives.

A GOLFER'S
ESSENTIAL READING

This is a very personal list, a reflection more on my own values and interests than on the game of golf. But if you find even one book here to touch your golfer's heart, I will be quite satisfied.

THE HOLY BIBLE BOOK OF PROVERBS

This isn't at the top of the list for most golf libraries, and I'll admit that I've read it through completely only once in my life. That one time was enough to leave me with enough thoughts, however, that I can call upon them under pressure. You don't have to be a particularly religious person nor a person of any specific faith to see the wisdom in Proverbs. Like the facets of our life, golf is something we can improve at by being at peace with ourselves. Proverbs can help us find that peace.

EYEWITNESS TO HISTORY EDITED BY JOHN CAREY

Here is a book filled with eyewitness accounts of some of the most amazing people and events in all of recorded history.

From the eruption of Mt. Vesuvius in 79 A.D. to the Battle of Agincourt in 1415 to Captain Scott's South Pole expedition in 1912. It is fascinating to see what people think of others as they strive for greatness and to read how people react under the most intense pressures. Here are a few lines from T. E. Lawrence, otherwise known as Lawrence of Arabia, written in 1918: "We opened fire on the head of their line when it showed itself beyond the houses. They turned two field guns upon us, for reply. The shrapnel was as usual over-fused, and passed safely above our heads. . . ." Talk about your poise under pressure.

BLOOD, TOIL, TEARS, AND SWEAT: THE SPEECHES OF WINSTON CHURCHILL EDITED BY DAVID CANNADINE

This is a collection of speeches made by Sir Winston Churchill, my all-time hero. In it you'll find motivation for countless situations. The title of the book comes from Churchill's first speech after being named the wartime prime minister. In that speech, Sir Winston told the people of Britain that he had "nothing to offer you but blood, toil, tears, and sweat." These are the very same things that golf demands of us. (Although hopefully not too much blood.) "You ask what is our aim?" says Churchill. "I can answer in one word: Victory—victory at all costs, victory in spite of all terror, victory, however long and hard the road may be. . . ." Powerful stuff from a powerful man, and a reminder as to how far determination can take us.

HARVEY PENICK'S LITTLE RED BOOK: LESSONS AND TEACHINGS FROM A LIFETIME IN GOLF BY HARVEY PENICK

This slender book of advice on the game of golf was put together from notes made over the years by the great golf teaching professional Harvey Penick. The beauty of this book is that while it is intended to improve the reader's game, it does so with almost the complete absence of technical advice. Mr. Penick understood that golf was more of a spiritual pursuit than a mechanical act. One of the more famous bits of advice in the book is the simple sentence, "Take dead aim." It's a simple reminder to the everyday player that in order to hit a shot toward a target, one must first aim very carefully at that target. Most poor golfers fail to do this seemingly obvious thing before reading this book, but not after.

THE TRAGEDY OF MACBETH
BY WILLIAM SHAKESPEARE

You may have read *Macbeth* in high school and see it listed here and think there is no way you'd put yourself through reading it again. What you might not remember is that *Macbeth* is actually quite a short work that is good fun to read. The reason it is good for the golfer is that our game offers no short cuts—the only way to success is the long way. *Macbeth* reminds us of what happens when we try to take the easy way out. Beyond that, it reminds us of the penalties of cheating. Who will be the wiser if you give your ball a little nudge with your foot when no one is looking? You will, and as Macbeth and his Lady find out, chicanery is not a good thing to have on one's conscience.

THE GOLF OMNIBUS
BY P. G. WODEHOUSE

There is no denying that the frustration that golf can bring about can at times reach such levels of absurdity that all we can do is laugh. The easiest and most enjoyable reading on the game of golf are the short stories of Sir P. G. Wodehouse. They are especially useful after a round in which things don't go as we had hoped. With Wodehouse's cast of characters— the Oldest Member, the Wrecking Crew, Chester, George Macintosh—you'll be surrounded by golfers who on their best days are worse than you ever feared being. Give Mr. Wodehouse a chance to brighten your day, and you'll be hooked on him for life.

THE DOGGED VICTIMS
OF INEXORABLE FATE
BY DAN JENKINS

On the subject of laughter, here is a collection of short and hysterically funny accounts by the master sportswriter Dan Jenkins. The thing you must remember about Jenkins is that he was quite a good golfer in his day, and he really understands the game far more than most golf writers. Still, he does not wear his knowledge like a gaudy sweater. He uses it for tweaking the game's great players and events and also for writing about the game as the weekend player knows it. What could be better than the combination of sharp insights and humor?

If
BY RUDYARD KIPLING

Do you remember this from your days as a schoolboy? It's the great poem by the man they called the Bard of the Empire. Almost everyone knows the famous line about how "If you can keep your head when all about you are losing theirs and blaming it on you . . ." That is only the first line of this timeless advice for life, however. In the middle of the poem, we are told:

> If you can force your heart and nerve and sinew
>
> To serve your turn long after they are gone
>
> And so hold on when there is nothing in you
>
> Except the Will which says to them, 'Hold on!' . . .

This is the essence of golf, the game that forces us to do everything on our own with help from no one else.

Goals

**WHY YOU CAN'T GET WHERE YOU'RE
GOING IF YOU DON'T PLAN THE WAY**

There are countless ways in which the elements of golf are used as metaphors for the challenges and opportunities of everyday life. Seldom, however, do I see or hear expressed what I believe the game teaches us about how we approach our lives in the long term. But therein may lie golf's greatest lesson.

The world is filled with what I refer to as dreamers and doers. Dreamers don't do anything to achieve their goals, whereas doers are dreamers with a difference—those who are willing to make the necessary sacrifices to achieve success. Doers are willing to break through the barriers of pain that stand between themselves and a goal. The pain barriers might be emotional or physical—or both. Doers realize that any goal of substance is not meant to be achieved easily and that they will face severe tests of their patience and determination along the path to fulfillment.

In the summer of 2000, I went to St. Andrews, Scotland, for the Open Championship. There I saw the ultimate doer, Tiger Woods, in action. That week in July was a big one for young Mr. Woods. This particular Open Championship was the only one of golf's four major championships that had eluded him. Winning it would put him in a small club of champions who had won each of the majors at least once—the career Grand Slam. At the time, that club consisted only of Gene Sarazen, Ben Hogan, Jack Nicklaus, and myself.

The typical competitor arrives at the tournament site for a championship a few days before the first round, which is typically a Thursday. Tiger Woods was in St. Andrews for the *entire week* prior to

the week of the Open. By the time I arrived on the
Monday before the Open, he was many days into
his preparation. On the day I arrived, I checked into
my hotel at around noontime, and as I looked out
the window of my room I saw Tiger walking down
the first fairway of the Old Course. I then went off
for lunch and then to the practice range before
heading out for a practice round myself. As I played
my round, I looked behind me at one point, and
there was Tiger, playing his second practice round
of the day. After I finished my round, I went back to
the hotel to clean up and change for dinner. As I did
so, I once again looked out the window and once
again saw Tiger coming down the 17th fairway of
the Old Course. The fact that he practices by himself and that the summer sunlight in the British Isles
lasts long into the evening meant that he had plenty
of time for another round. It was the end of his
second practice round in a single day. Later that
night, he put in a full workout at the gym.

When a person is capable of playing golf at

the level Tiger Woods does, it is not necessary to play two rounds of golf in a single day in order to keep the golf swing finely honed. What, you may wonder, was Tiger doing? The answer is that he was mapping his way toward his goal. The end goal of the week was to be standing outside the old Royal and Ancient clubhouse holding the silver claret jug awarded to the Open Champion. Between Tiger and that goal were more than 150 other superb golfers. To get where he was headed, Tiger had to break down every possible barrier of pain. To play two rounds of golf for a man as fit as he is did not constitute physical torture. It does tax one's patience and perseverance, however.

In playing the Old Course over and over again, Tiger Woods was poking it and prodding it to find its weak spots and strengths. There would be no point at which he would face a shot where he was uncertain as to how to proceed. Because he had outworked everyone else in the field, he would know where the course was vulnerable and where

he could attack it. He would also know when to respect the course and make a more conservative play.
His diligence removed doubt from his mind.

In watching him, I was reminded of a friend of
mine who is the manager of a large group of sales-
people. He always told his employees that there
was never any excuse for being late to an appointment, most especially getting lost when in an unfa-
miliar area. He reasoned that if you wanted to make
the sale badly enough, you would get into town the
day before the appointment and drive to the place
where the appointment would be. That way you
could be certain you wouldn't get lost.

Every round of golf we play teaches us the importance of having a goal and also having a logical
plan for achieving that goal. Before the start of a
round, our goal is to shoot the lowest possible
score. To do that we will have to play 18 holes, each
an entity unto itself, yet each contributing to the
end goal. Each of those 18 holes requires a goal and
a plan. The goal is to get the ball in the hole in the
fewest number of strokes, and our plan to do that is

to make sure each shot leaves us in the perfect position to play the subsequent shot. As such, we work in reverse from our goal. We see where the hole is located on the green and determine the best angle from which to approach that position. In order to reach the spot that affords us the best possible angle to the hole, we have to play one or two shots to put us in the proper place. We have to plot the way before we begin the advance toward the goal.

Things do not always go as we expect in golf. The plan sometimes goes awry in the form of a bad shot. When it does, it is easy to lose site of the end goal—the lowest score for the round—and convince ourselves that we must do something dramatic in order to rescue the situation on the hole we are playing. This most often leads to foolish decisions and players attempting to play shots beyond their skill levels. As the strokes start to mount, the end goal moves further and further away. Our patience and determination get tested.

Troublesome situations on the golf course demand patience. The right decision in such moments is to get the ball safely back into play and work for some good chances later in the round.

Learn from this. Let your determination be your guide during troublesome times. If you want to do something badly enough, have the patience to realize that a minor setback on the road to the end goal is just that: minor. By ensuring that the minor situation does not escalate into a major one, we keep our hope of achieving our goal alive. And in time, we usually persevere.

As for Tiger Woods, he not only won that Open Championship by eight strokes, but he had the lowest tournament score ever recorded there.

Change

THE NEW LIFE IN

THE INEVITABLE PROCESS

All golfers are familiar with the term *mulligan*. While it is, strictly speaking, against the Rules of Golf, a first-tee mulligan for the weekend player offers the chance to get his day started under more enjoyable circumstances. If it's not a serious competition and all the players in a group agree on mulligans, then there is no harm done to the game.

As a professional golfer, of course, mulligans are out of the question. I was able to understand the joy found in a mulligan, however, when I turned 50 and started playing golf on the Senior PGA Tour. It was the mulligan of life for me, and it was a great reward in the sense that since I knew I had always given my best, I was now about to experience something new without any regrets.

I have to admit that this change came with a few self-acknowledgments that were not the easiest things to accept. Foremost among these was the fact that I could no longer compete at the very pinnacle of the game. I could still play well, but those rounds that at one time were routinely 67s and 68s were consistently becoming rounds of 71s or 72s. In the highly competitive world of professional golf, that seemingly small difference is equivalent to the difference between an anthill and Mt. Everest. An inevitable change had come for me, and with it came the flood of thoughts that always accompany change.

When I thought about how much money I could have made if the peak years of my career had occurred during the current time, it was staggering. I'm fairly certain that with the improvements in equipment, course conditioning, and the prize money contested for these days, I could have easily made $50 million in prize money. When I first started playing, the equipment was certainly better than that used by players who had preceded me in professional golf, but it was very difficult to use in comparison to modern high-tech clubs and balls. The golf courses we played on in the 1960s and 1970s were practically cow pastures compared to today's. When I thought about those things, I could see how it would have been easy for me to be bitter toward, and even jealous of, today's young players.

Rather than focus on those things, however, I decided I would do two things: First, I would treasure the experiences and the joys of my early career as something that the modern player would and could never know. Second, I decided I would enjoy what I was now presented with, rather than abhor it.

I'm not one who is big on looking back, but I realize now that when presented with changes in life, it is very healthy to take a little time to recall where we've been and how the things that happened to us are ours and ours alone. For all of his talent, Tiger Woods will never know the sheer joy of playing a competitive round of golf on a course nearly devoid of spectators. I can recall times playing tournaments in Australia where the ground was so dry the fairways had huge cracks in them. A handful of people would wander out to watch not because they were golf fans, but rather because they were delighted just to see other people. They were truly thrilled simply because we were there.

A young player today probably will never know the gratification that comes with the struggle of being nearly broke, of spending everything you have just to get to tournaments, or of renting a small bedroom in an old house in England for 15 shillings a night and having the woman who owns the house greet you with a cup of tea and pleasant conversation when you return home in the evening. A player today wouldn't know what to do if he had to travel by train, but it was a fun and adventurous thing. And he'll never know the delight of arriving at the course to find his caddie looking smart in a shirt and tie and all the other decorum that has vanished with the passing of time. To know that I have those treasures in my mind and can unlock them any time I choose is to know that I have something no one else can exactly replicate.

The fear of change is really the fear of the unknown, and man knows no greater fear than that of the unknown. It always strikes me as odd that people get consumed by this fear of change because, when you think about it, every day we're alive is unknown to us before we live it. This is why I think it is useful to occasionally take the time to look back on where we've been, and in doing so realize that before we did those things—whatever they were—they were unknown to us. Before we did them, they represented change to us because they forced us out of our comfort zone. But when we look back at them, we realize that there was nothing at all to fear in these changes, and that in fact they provided us the most wonderful moments of our life.

As more and more change enters my life, I have vowed to accept it for what it truly is: opportunity. As we get older, there is a tendency to view life as offering us less and less opportunity to do things. That is a worthless notion. When my playing skills diminished, I knew I would need something more than just playing golf on the Senior Tour. That competition would satisfy my yearning to compete, but it would not fulfill my desire to continue learning and trying new things. That's when I decided to get heavily involved in designing golf courses. For certain, there was a monetary factor involved in my design work, but I had more than enough money by that time. The true value for me came in finding that even with the change in my golf game, I could still do something within the game that would give me a sense of purpose and fulfill my desire to be productive. As a result, I have literally built golf courses all over the world—from the Americas, Canada, Puerto Rico, and Europe to Africa, Israel, the Philippines, Japan, and Australia—and then some. Along the way, I have made new friends and found new satisfactions that had previously been unknown to me.

Fear the unknown? Go ahead if you like. Not me. To fear it is to never know the wonder of new-found things.

The Game Eternal

HOW GOLF WILL

NEVER LET YOU DOWN

At the 1978 Masters Tournament, I was 42 years old. It had been nearly 20 years since I won the Open Championship at Muirfield in Scotland. On that Sunday in Augusta, Georgia, I was playing one of the very finest rounds of my career, yet the spectators seemed indifferent to it. It wasn't that they didn't like me; it was simply a matter of that they felt I was too old to make a serious run at the title. I was playing with the then-very-young Seve Ballesteros from Spain. I turned to him and said, "You know, Seve, these people don't think I can win. You watch. I'll show them that I can."

The truth is that it was not the lack of interest shown by the spectators in what I was doing that stuck in my craw. It was the logic they used to arrive at their state of mind toward me. They thought I was over the hill. To be honest, that anyone would think that infuriated me. In the end, I shot a round of 64 and won the title. It was a very gratifying moment, not because I felt I had "shown them" (the crowd), but rather because I hoped it demonstrated to everyone watching that golf is the most glorious of all games, because as long as you can draw a breath, it can be played and played well.

In that moment of realization when I said those words to Seve, I realized that golf was giving me back, all at once, all of the things that I had put into it. It was presenting me a challenge, and it was providing me with motivation. It was giving me the opportunity to show my determination and that I could still outwork and outthink other players. It was allowing me to demonstrate that there is always something new to be learned and that we are capable of achieving anything once we put our minds to it. Because I had kept my body in shape my entire life, I was still able to answer the call to battle, and my mind was still sharp enough to handle the pressure because my body had prepared it to do so. What a moment! The whole of life and the game I loved compressed into an instant in time.

What happened to me that day at Augusta National could not have happened if all those years before I had not decided on golf as my passion. Who knows why, in that moment when I was a teenager and realized we all need some passion, that I had decided golf would be mine? Unbeknownst to me at that time, I had made a choice to play a game that would move me in ways I could not fathom, a game that would exact the fullest measure of the man from within me. Who knew that my mind and my soul and my body and all that goes with those things would be tested in a manner that so few passions offer? Who knew the rewards the game would bring me: the delicious feeling of the well-struck shot surging up the shaft of the club and through my body; the renewed zest for life that accompanied each morning on the golf course when all was quiet and I could feel my small place in this big world; the self-acknowledgment that whatever happened during that day depended on me and me alone—that there would be no one to blame, no excuses that could be conjured up? Every day, I knew, was an examination of myself, not how well I knew the mechanics of swinging the golf club or the subtleties of putting, or how crafty I was when playing from the sand. Rather, it was a look deep inside of me, to see if I had the stuff to be honest and true to myself.

This game of ours—this confounding game— offers the things I have described to all players of every level. To know the feeling of the purely struck shot, one does not have to play in the U.S. Open. To know the glory of the quiet morning on the golf course or of the lonely round on the windswept links alongside the ocean, one does not have to compete in the Open Championship. The best part of all of this is that golf offers us the most enjoyable social circumstances of any game. You most often play the game in the company of others—but you are not trying to beat them as much as you are trying to tame yourself. As such, you are presented with a neat opportunity to spend time with friends while at the same time discover yourself. The game is simultaneously social and solitary, and it stays that way from the moment you first swing a club until the end of your days on this planet.

My point here is that golf is, of course, only a game. But it is a game that loves you back. I know of no man, woman, or child that ever felt as if the game somehow let them down. It may at times challenge us more than we would like it to, but does not life do the same? And do we not find when the challenge is greatest on the golf course that if we work our hardest, the challenge is overcome? We do, just as we do in life. We who play the game also know that sometimes we get pleasant and unexpected surprises, such as a hole-in-one or a ball that skips off the water and onto dry land. We also know we are equally likely to get a bad break—a wild bounce of the ball, a sudden gust of wind. The game leaves us no choice but to accept the good with the bad and to move on to the next shot. In other words, we take what the game deals us, and we do the best we can moving forward. That's the way life is, and the grand old game of golf will never let you forget it.